Simply soups
for summer and winter

Editorial director: Brigitte Éveno

Design and layout: Guylaine & Christophe Moi

Production: Caroline Artémon

Editorial assistant: Sylvie Gauthier

Translation by Laura Washburn for JMS Books LLP

Design UK edition Chris Bell

The editors would like to thank Maïté Lapierre for her invaluable assistance

Simply soups
for summer and winter

Sophie Brissaud

Photographs by Jean-Blaise Hall
Styling by Valérie Lhomme

acknowledgements

Valérie Lhomme would like to thank
the following suppliers who kindly lent
props: Quartz, La Forge Subtile, Monastica
and Blanc d'Ivoire. She would also like to
thank Alice, Tristan, Victor and Philippe,
who accepted the invitation to come along
one Wednesday and sample some of the
soups under the skillful eye of Jean-Blaise
Hall's camera.

contents

summer soups 7

    recipe list 7

    introduction 8

    summer recipes 10

    helpful hints for summer 24

winter soups 51

    recipe list 51

    introduction 52

    winter recipes 54

    helpful hints for winter 68

index of recipes 95

summer soups

recipe list

Cream of cucumber with mint	10
Jellied beetroot consommé	12
Vichyssoise with watercress	14
Creamy Mexican courgette soup	17
Provençal vegetable soup (soupe au pistou)	18
Chilled rocket soup	20
Strawberry soup with balsamic vinegar	22
Normandy apple and potato soup	26
Andalucian hake soup	28
Greek egg soup with lemon	31
Hungarian chicken and white grape soup	32
Almond gazpacho	33
Hungarian sour cherry soup	34
French fish soup (bourride)	36
Senegalese prawn soup with coconut	39
Indian tomato soup	41
Creamy pear soup with blue cheese	42
Brazilian sweet potato soup	44
Mango and melon soup	46
Ivory Coast avocado soup	48

introduction

The weather's fine and a warm breeze is blowing. Perhaps the leaves are gently rustling, or there's a distant sound of waves crashing on the shore. It's a time to be lazy, but that's no reason to stop entertaining. And a chilled soup is the perfect way to begin a relaxing meal with friends. These soups are easily made in advance and kept in the refrigerator until serving, adding a touch of refined elegance to a balmy summer feast.

Chilled soups are not a new invention, they have been around for ages, we are only just rediscovering them. They have long been popular in southern and eastern European countries, where these refreshing delicacies are savoured slowly, to combat the stifling heat. What a delicious way to cool down, with a cold consommé, a creamy chilled soup or a sparkling jellied treat. Warm soups also contribute to a summer menu. These are lighter and more invigorating than their cold-weather counterparts, filled with sun-gorged ingredients and more adventurous flavours, such as fruit or sweet-and-sour. For the most part, warm summer soups work just as well served chilled, however, the reverse is not always possible, since cold soups often rely on uncooked ingredients for their character.

Cream of cucumber with mint

- Bring 200 ml (7 fl oz) water to the boil in a small saucepan. Add the stock cube and stir to dissolve. Set aside to cool.
- Wash and shred the mint sprigs. Wash and peel the cucumbers in stripes, leaving some skin intact. Cut in half lengthways and scoop out the seeds. Slice into a large bowl.
- In a food processor or blender, purée the cucumber slices with the mint, dill, stock, whipping cream and sugar, working in batches if necessary. Transfer to a large bowl and mix well. Season with pepper, cover and refrigerate for at least 2 hours.
- To serve, taste for seasoning, then ladle into chilled bowls, adding a dollop of crème fraîche to each one. Garnish with cucumber slices and chives.

Serves 4-6
Preparation: 30 minutes
Refrigeration: at least
2 hours

1 chicken stock cube
7–8 sprigs fresh mint
2 firm cucumbers
3 sprigs fresh dill
200 ml (7 fl oz) whipping cream
3 teaspoons sugar
salt and freshly ground white pepper
6 tablespoons crème fraîche
a few chives, extra cucumber slices, for garnish

Jellied beetroot consommé

• Peel and wash the beetroot, then cut into cubes. Put in a saucepan with about 500 ml (17 fl oz) water and bring to the boil, then lower the heat, cover and simmer gently for 40 minutes. Drain, reserving the cooking liquid, and set to one side.

• Add the stock, vinegar, celery seeds and dried dill to the beetroot cooking liquid. Bring to the boil, then lower the heat and simmer for 10 minutes. Taste for seasoning.

• Strain the broth through a coffee filter. Season with pepper. Add the gelatine sheets and stir gently until dissolved. Add the beetroot cubes, cover and refrigerate until thick and syrupy. Stir well, cover and refrigerate again until set.

• To serve, break up the jelly with a spoon and divide amongst serving bowls. Top each with a dollop of yogurt, snipped chives and slices of lemon.

Serves 4
Preparation: 25 minutes
Cooking time: 35 minutes
Refrigeration: 6 hours

2 beetroot, uncooked
500 ml (17 fl oz) vegetable or beef stock
1 tablespoon red wine vinegar
pinch celery seeds
pinch dried dill
6 gelatine sheets
4 tablespoons thick Greek yogurt
1 bunch chives
1 lemon
salt and freshly ground white pepper

Vichyssoise with watercress

• Peel and wash the potatoes, then cut into cubes. Peel the garlic. Choose a few leafy watercress sprigs and set aside, then chop the rest without untying the bunch, close to the stems. Wash and dry thoroughly.

• In a large saucepan, combine two-thirds of the chopped watercress, the potatoes, garlic and stock. Bring to the boil, then lower the heat, cover and simmer gently for 20 minutes. Purée in a food processor or blender, then return to the pan. Stir in the whipping cream, season, and bring just to simmering point, then remove from the heat. Taste for seasoning, cover and set aside.

• Combine most of the reserved watercress leaves and the crème fraîche in a small food processor or blender and purée. Stir the delicate green cream into the soup, cover and allow to stand until lukewarm. Refrigerate for at least 2 hours.

• To serve, taste for seasoning, then ladle into bowls and decorate with a swirl of whipping cream and a few watercress sprigs.

Serves 4-6
Preparation: 30 minutes
Cooking time: 20 minutes
Refrigeration: 2 hours

4–5 new potatoes
1 garlic clove
2 bunches watercress
700 ml (1¼ pints) chicken stock
300 ml (½ pint) whipping cream
4 tablespoons crème fraîche
salt and freshly ground white pepper

Creamy Mexican courgette soup

Serves 4
Preparation:
30 minutes
Cooking time:
40 minutes
Refrigeration:
at least 6 hours

4 young, firm courgettes
2 tablespoons chopped coriander
1 small onion
2 tablespoons clarified butter
1 tablespoon flour
200 ml (7 fl oz) evaporated milk or whipping cream
200 ml (7 fl oz) chicken stock
salt and freshly ground pepper
courgette flowers, to garnish (optional)

• Wash and scrub the courgettes, then cut into large pieces. Put them in a saucepan with enough cold water to cover. Bring to the boil, cover and simmer gently for 20 minutes. Remove from the heat and allow to stand, uncovered until lukewarm.

• In a food processor, combine the courgettes, 200 ml (7 fl oz) of their cooking liquid and the coriander. Process until smooth.

• Peel and chop the onion finely. Heat the butter in a saucepan, add the onion and cook over low heat until soft, about 15 minutes. Add the flour, stir well, then stir in the courgette purée, the evaporated milk or cream and the stock. Whisk gently to combine. Season and bring to a gentle simmer: do not allow to boil.

• Remove from the heat and allow to cool, then refrigerate for at least 6 hours. To serve, garnish with coriander sprigs and courgette flowers, if available.

• This soup can also be served hot.

Serves 6
Preparation: 40 minutes
Cooking time: 1 hour 40 minutes
Soaking time: 12 hours

100g (3½ oz) white or kidney beans • ½ teaspoon bicarbonate of soda • 1 onion •
6 large garlic cloves, inner green shoots removed • 2 turnips • 2 carrots • 1 small
celery stick • 3 ripe tomatoes • 200 ml (7 fl oz) olive oil • 1 bouquet garni (thyme,
bay leaf, savory) • 1 small slice of pumpkin or squash • 2 small courgettes • handful
fine green beans • 2 leeks, white part only • 1 small bunch flat leaf parsley • 1 large
bunch basil, with large leaves • 50 g (2 oz) pine kernels • 50 g (2 oz) grated Parmesan
(or Pecorino) • large handful (or more if desired) small pasta shapes, such as
macaroni • salt and freshly ground pepper

Provençal vegetable soup (soupe au pistou)

• Soak the beans overnight in enough cold water to cover, with the bicarbonate of soda. The following day, drain, put in a pan, cover with fresh water and cook until tender, 30–40 minutes. Drain.

• Chop the onion, 2 of the garlic cloves, the turnips, carrots and celery into small cubes. Peel, de-seed and chop the tomatoes.

• Heat some of the olive oil in a large saucepan. Add the onion, garlic, carrots, celery, turnip and drained beans and cook gently for a few minutes. Add the tomatoes and generously cover with cold water. Bring to the boil and season lightly. Add the bouquet garni, lower the heat, cover and simmer gently for 40 minutes.

• Meanwhile, cube the peeled pumpkin and courgettes and slice the green beans into short pieces. Slice the leek whites and chop the parsley. Wash and dry the basil.

• To make the pistou, peel the remaining garlic cloves. Place in a mortar and pestle with the pine kernels, basil and Parmesan, and crush. Gradually add the remaining olive oil to obtain a thick paste. Set aside.

• Add the leeks, pumpkin, courgettes, green beans, pasta and parsley to the soup. Taste for seasoning, adding more water if necessary. Simmer gently for 15 minutes. Just before serving, stir in the pistou.

Variation: In Provence, 2 ripe, peeled, de-seeded and chopped tomatoes are sometimes added to the pistou.

Chilled rocket soup

- Wash and dry the rocket and remove any stems. Set aside one handful and chop finely.
- Coarsely chop the white part of the spring onions. Heat the olive oil in a saucepan, add the onions and cook for 2 minutes. Add the whole rocket leaves and half the stock. Bring to the boil, then lower the heat and simmer gently for 1–2 minutes, until the rocket just begins to wilt, then transfer to a food processor or blender and purée. Return to the pan, add the remaining stock and simmer gently for 2 minutes; do not allow to boil. Remove from the heat and stir in the cream and chopped rocket. Season with salt and pepper. Cover and refrigerate for at least 2 hours.
- Cook the eggs until hard-boiled. Peel under cold, running water and allow to cool. Chop the yolks and one of the whites. Snip the chives and stir in, salt lightly and set aside.
- To serve, ladle into bowls or tall glasses and garnish with the egg and chive mixture and thyme flowers.

Serves 4
Preparation: 40 minutes
Cooking time: 4 minutes
Refrigeration time: at least 2 hours

300 g (10 oz) fresh rocket
4 spring onions
2 tablespoons olive oil
750 ml (1¼ pints) chicken stock
200 ml (7 fl oz) whipping cream
2 eggs
a few fresh chives
salt and freshly ground pepper
a few fresh thyme flowers, to garnish

Strawberry soup with balsamic vinegar

• Lightly rinse the strawberries and remove the stems. Choose 20 of the best ones, cut them in half and sprinkle with half the sugar and 2 tablespoons of the balsamic vinegar. Refrigerate for 2 hours.

• Combine the remaining strawberries, sugar, vinegar, orange and lemon peel in a food processor, together with the Grand Marnier or orange juice, and purée. Transfer to a large bowl and stir well until the sugar is completely dissolved. Whisk in the yogurt. Refrigerate for 2 hours.

• Serve in shallow bowls, garnished with the marinated strawberry halves and a few drizzles of the marinade.

• This dish makes a delicious starter, but can also be served as a dessert.

Serves 4–6
Preparation:
20 minutes
Marinating time:
at least 2 hours

1 kg (2 lb) ripe, sweet strawberries, such as French gariguette (or use Alpine strawberries)

200 g (7 oz) caster sugar

6 tablespoons balsamic vinegar from Modena

1/2 teaspoon finely grated orange peel (from an organic orange)

1/2 teaspoon finely grated lemon peel (from an organic lemon)

1 tablespoon Grand Marnier (or use orange juice)

500 ml (17 fl oz) thick Greek yogurt

Helpful hints
for summer

For most of these recipes, you will need stock or water. Here are some guidelines for preparing simple, basic stocks and enhancing them according to taste and available ingredients.

• **Vegetable stock:** carrots, turnips, leeks, onions, garlic, celery or celeriac, herbs, whole peppercorns can all be combined; you could add flat leaf parsley, parsnip, tomato, fennel, beetroot (this will give you a deep red stock), cabbage, etc. Cover the vegetables and herbs with plenty of cold water, salt lightly and bring to the boil. Lower the heat and simmer gently for 1½ hours. Strain.

• **Fish stock:** use the bones and heads from white fish (flat fish such as sole or plaice are ideal) and add carrots, onion, shallots, leek whites, herbs, whole peppercorns, a splash of white wine and some fennel seeds. Bring to the boil, add salt, then simmer gently for 30 minutes. Strain well before using.

• Delicate and refined ingredients have different stock requirements: do not use stocks that are so strong as to overpower the soup (cold soups, however, may need stronger stock for fuller flavours). When using water, be sure to use filtered or spring water whenever possible.

• Locally grown produce is readily available in summer than in winter, so take advantage of the seasonal glut. Be sure to buy everything as fresh as possible, and use quickly for optimum flavour and nutritional value. In an ideal world, keep fresh produce out of the refrigerator. The cold hardens peas, makes asparagus woody, spoils mushrooms and strips strawberries of their flavour. Buy fresh and cook soon after purchase. Take care to let chilled soups cool to room temperature before refrigerating.

Normandy apple and potato soup

• Slice the leeks. Peel the tart apples and the potatoes and cut into cubes.

• Heat 4 tablespoons of the butter in a large saucepan, add the leeks and cook to soften, about 3 minutes. Add the apple cubes, cook for 5 more minutes, stirring often, then add the potatoes and stock. Bring to the boil, lower the heat, cover and simmer gently for 40 minutes.

• Transfer to a food processor or blender and purée. Stir in the cream and cinnamon. Season with salt and pepper, then cover and refrigerate for at least 2 hours.

• Peel and dice the firm-fleshed apples, then cook in the remaining butter until golden, for about 5 minutes, stirring often.

• Serve the soup in bowls, garnished with the apple cubes and a dash of Calvados, if using.

• This soup can also be served hot.

Serves 4–6
Preparation: 30 minutes
Cooking time: 40 minutes
Refrigeration: at least
2 hours

2 leeks, white part only
1 kg (2 lb) tart eating apples,
such as Granny Smith or Cox
2 new potatoes
6 tablespoons clarified butter
1.5 litres (2½ pints) chicken stock
250 ml (8 fl oz) double cream
pinch of ground cinnamon
2 firm-fleshed apples, such as
Braeburn
salt and freshly ground white
pepper
Calvados, for serving (optional)

Andalucian hake soup

• Cut the hake into slices about 7 cm (3 inches) thick. Salt generously and allow to stand for 1 hour.

• Peel the garlic. Trim the crust from the bread and cut into cubes. Cook the bread cubes in 100 ml (3½ fl oz) of the olive oil, then rub with 2 garlic cloves. Set aside and keep warm.

• Heat the remaining oil in a large saucepan and gently fry the remaining whole garlic cloves. As soon as they begin to turn golden, add the onion and cook over low heat for 1 minute. Do not allow the onion brown. Add 1.5 litres (2½ pints) boiling water, cover and simmer gently for 20 minutes. Raise the heat, add the hake pieces, one at a time, maintaining a constant boil. Cook for 15 minutes over medium heat. You can cook the fish for a shorter time, but the broth will have less flavour.

• Just before serving, stir in the orange juice. Serve in a heated terracotta tureen, with the croutons. Aïoli (garlic mayonnaise) goes well with this dish, though it is not traditional.

Serves 4–6
Preparation: 20 minutes
Cooking time: 35 minutes
Standing time: 1 hour

1 kg (2 lb) hake (1 or 2, depending on size), gutted and scaled

10 large garlic cloves

6 slices rustic sourdough bread, such as Poilâne

300 ml (½ pint) olive oil

1 large onion, finely chopped

150 ml (¼ pint) bitter orange juice (or the juice of 1 lime and 1 clementine)

Aïoli (optional, see page 34)

salt

Serves 4–6
Preparation: 30 minutes
Cooking time: 20 minutes
Refrigeration: 6 hours

1.5 litres (2¹/₂ pints) chicken stock • **pinch ground allspice** • **small pinch of ground cayenne** • **3 level tablespoons long grain rice** • **4 large fresh eggs** • **juice of 3 lemons** • **6 lemon slices** • **grated nutmeg** • **salt and freshly ground white pepper**

Greek egg soup with lemon

• Put the stock in a large saucepan with the allspice and the cayenne. Bring to the boil and add the rice. Lower the heat and cook for 15 minutes; the rice should be tender on the outside but still slightly firm to the bite. Turn the heat down as low as possible.

• Beat the eggs vigorously, as if making an omelette. Gradually whisk in the lemon juice; the mixture will lighten in colour. Add 1 ladleful of the simmering stock to the egg mixture, whisking constantly. Add another ladleful and then a third, still whisking. Pour the egg and stock mixture into the pan. Return just to a simmering point, stirring gently; do not allow it to boil. As soon as the soup thickens, remove from the heat. Taste for seasoning.

• Cover and allow to cool. Refrigerate for at least 6 hours. Serve chilled, garnished with lemon slices and a sprinkling of fresh grated nutmeg.

Variation: For a smooth, creamy consistency, purée the soup after adding the egg and lemon mixture.

Hungarian chicken and white grape soup

Serves 6-8
Preparation: 1 hour
Cooking time about 2 hours

36 large Italian seeded white grapes •
1 parsnip • 1 small celeriac • 3 carrots
• 1 small onion • 1 large free-range
chicken (about 1 kg/2 lb) • 1 bouquet
garni (4 sprigs flat leaf parsley, 1 leafy
end of a celery stick, 1 thyme sprig) •
250 ml (8 fl oz) sweet white wine,
such as Jurançon, Loupiac or Mon-
bazillac • 2 organic lemons, halved •
3 sugar cubes • 2 tablespoons flour •
1 tablespoon chicken or duck fat •
4 tablespoons crème fraîche • salt and
freshly ground white pepper

• Peel and de-seed the grapes, cover and set
aside. Peel all the vegetables and dice finely.

• Put the chicken into a large saucepan and add
2.5 litres (4 pints) of water and some salt. Bring
to a simmer, then add a splash of cold water to
prevent boiling. Skim, then repeat this process
three times. Add the bouquet garni and the
vegetables. Cook over low heat until the
chicken is tender, about 1½ hours.

• Remove the bouquet garni. Take out the
chicken, dice all the meat and set aside. Strain
the stock and set aside, keeping several carrot
cubes for garnish. Put the wine in a saucepan,
add the lemons and sugar and bring to the boil.
Boil for 10 minutes. Remove the lemons and
squeeze all their juice into the wine, discard the
lemon halves. Add the grapes to the warm wine,
cover and allow to stand for 5 minutes.

• Heat the poultry fat in a pan and add the
flour. Cook gently until the mixture just begins
to turn golden. Add a few spoonfuls of stock
and stir well, then pour this roux into the
reserved stock, stirring well. Add the diced
chicken and boil for 5 minutes.

• Before serving, stir in the wine mixture and
the crème fraîche. Taste for seasoning and serve
with a sweet wine.

Serves 4-6
Preparation: 45 minutes
Refrigeration: about 2 hours

4 slices of white bread, crusts removed • 200 g (7 oz) large
white seeded grapes • 2 large garlic cloves • 200 g (7 oz)
blanched almonds • 1–2 tablespoons red wine vinegar •
180 ml (6 fl oz) extra virgin olive oil • handful slivered
almonds • salt and freshly ground pepper

Almond gazpacho

• Break up the bread slices and reduce to fine breadcrumbs in a food processor. Allow to soak in water for 30 minutes. Peel the grapes, cut in half and remove the pips. Put in a bowl, cover and set aside. Squeeze the breadcrumbs dry with your hands. Peel the garlic and remove any green sprouts from the centre.

• Combine the breadcrumbs, garlic, blanched almonds, vinegar and oil in a food processor. Process until smooth. Transfer to a salad bowl and refrigerate for 2 hours.

• Before serving, dilute with water to the desired consistency. Season with salt and pepper and add the grapes. Garnish with the slivered almonds and serve with chilled white wine.

Hungarian sour cherry soup

• Stone the cherries and set aside the flesh. Put the stones in a saucepan with enough water to cover. Bring to the boil, then lower the heat and simmer gently for 30 minutes. Strain and measure the liquid. You will need 1.5 litres (2½ pints), so add water as necessary to make up the quantity. Set aside.

• In a bowl, stir together the crème fraîche, flour, salt and icing sugar to obtain a thick paste. Set aside.

• Put the cherry pieces in a saucepan and add the stones' cooking-liquid. Add the caster sugar and bring to the boil, then lower the heat and simmer for 20 minutes. Transfer 2 ladlefuls of the cherry liquid to the crème fraîche paste and whisk for 2 minutes, then pour this crème fraîche mixture into the soup, stir well and add the cinnamon, if using. Simmer, uncovered, for 5 minutes, then remove from the heat, cover and allow to cool. Taste for seasoning; you should be able to detect a slight salty taste.

• This is a traditional Hungarian recipe, always served chilled, and always as a starter. The cherry stones add a seductive bitterness, but they can be omitted.

Serves 6
Preparation: 50 minutes
Cooking time: 55 minutes

500 g (1 lb) sour cherries
(or any available variety)
250 ml (8 fl oz) crème fraîche
2 level tablespoons flour
1 teaspoon icing sugar
200 g (7 oz) caster sugar
2 pinches ground cinnamon
(optional)
pinch of salt

French fish soup (bourride)

- Cut the fish into thick slices. Season lightly and squeeze over some lemon juice. Set aside.
- Peel the potatoes and cook in salted water until tender. Set aside in their cooking liquid to keep warm.
- Put the fish stock into a large saucepan, add 1 sliced leek white, 1 lemon slice, the thyme, parsley stalks, bay leaf and vinegar. Bring to the boil, then simmer gently for 25 minutes. Strain and set aside.
- To make the aïoli, peel the 4 garlic cloves and remove any green sprouts from the centres. Mix with the breadcrumbs and crush with a pestle and mortar.

Serves 6
Preparation:
1 hour 30 minutes
Cooking time: 35 minutes

1 kg (2 lb) monkfish tail
(or halibut)
1–2 lemons
700 g (1½ lb) new potatoes
1.5 litres (2½ pints) fish stock
2 leeks, white part only
1 thyme sprig
1 bunch flat leaf parsley
1 bay leaf
1 tablespoon wine vinegar
1 garlic clove
2 tablespoons crème fraîche
salt and freshly ground pepper

- **For the aïoli:**
4 garlic cloves
1 tablespoon fine breadcrumbs
2–3 egg yolks
extra virgin olive oil
juice of ½ a lemon
salt and freshly ground pepper

Season with salt and pepper, add the egg yolks and mix well. Gradually add the oil, mixing well, and pouring slowly, as for mayonnaise, until you have about a bowlful. Squeeze in the juice of ½ lemon. Set aside.

- Heat some olive oil in a large pan. Add the remaining chopped leek white and the garlic clove, crushed. Put the fish pieces on top and add the stock. Bring slowly to the boil, then simmer gently for 10 minutes.
- Remove the fish pieces and put in a large soup tureen with the drained potatoes; keep warm. Reduce the fish stock by one-third. Stir in the crème fraîche and remove from the heat. Gradually incorporate the fish stock into the aïoli, a little at a time, whisking constantly, until it is all blended. The soup should thicken. Pour over the fish and serve immediately, garnished with chopped parsley.

Senegalese prawn soup with coconut

• Heat the butter in a heavy pan and add the onion. Cook over low heat until soft, about 10 minutes. Add the curry powder and flour and cook for 5 minutes more, stirring constantly. Add the coconut milk, then the stock, whisking until there are no more lumps. Simmer gently for 10 minutes, stirring occasionally.

• Whisk the egg yolks. Remove the soup from the heat and beat it into the eggs, little by little, whisking continously until fully incorporated. Return the mixture to a low heat and add the chicken and prawns. Cook until warmed through; do not allow to boil. Remove from the heat and taste for seasoning. Let cool, then refrigerate for at least 2 hours.

• Before serving, stir in the whipping cream. Serve well chilled, accompanied by cubes of pear and banana.

• This soup, which has Anglo-Indian origins, is very rich, so serve in small quantities.

Serves 4–6
Preparation: 25 minutes
Cooking time: 20 minutes
Refrigeration: at least
2 hours

2 tablespoons clarified butter
1 onion, finely chopped
2 teaspoons best quality curry powder
1 tablespoon flour
200 ml (7 fl oz) coconut milk
800 ml (1½ pints) strong chicken stock
2 egg yolks
100 g (3½ oz) cooked chicken breasts, diced
150 g (5 oz) frozen prawns, defrosted, shelled and coarsely chopped
500 ml (17 fl oz) whipping cream, chilled
1 firm ripe pear
1 banana
salt and freshly ground pepper

Indian tomato soup

Serves 4
Preparation:
35 minutes
Cooking time:
20 minutes

9 large garlic cloves
3 tablespoons clarified
butter or olive oil
pinch of coarsely ground
pepper
6 cloves
1 bay leaf
large pinch asafoetida
(available from Indian stores)
1 x 400 g (13 oz) tin peeled
tomatoes
1 level teaspoon turmeric
1 level teaspoon ground
fenugreek
$1/2$ teaspoon ground cumin
pinch ground chillies
2 sprigs curry leaves
1 tablespoon lime juice
1 chicken stock cube
(or 250 ml/8 fl oz strong
chicken stock)

• **For the garnish:**
$1/2$ teaspoon cumin seeds
1 teaspoon black mustard
seeds
1 teaspoon crushed urad dal
(small white lentils)
3 tablespoons chopped fresh
coriander

• Peel the garlic. Heat one-third of the butter and add 8 of the garlic cloves. Cook gently until golden all over. As soon as they begin to colour, add the coarse ground pepper, cloves and bay leaf. When they are well-coloured, add the asafoetida, tomatoes, all the ground spices, the curry leaves, lime juice, stock cube and 250 ml (8 fl oz) water (unless you are using stock). Bring to the boil, then cover, lower the heat and simmer gently for 20 minutes. Remove the curry leaves, bay leaf and cloves. Strain the soup through a sieve and return to a low heat, covered.

• To finish, slice the remaining garlic clove. Heat the rest of the butter, add the garlic slices, spices and lentils and cook over medium heat until golden. When the mustard seeds begin to pop, stir the mixture immediately into the soup. Stir well and add the coriander. Cover and allow to stand for 3 minutes before serving.

• This soup can also be served cold, but not chilled.

Serves 6–8
Preparation: 25 minutes
Cooking time: 80 minutes
Refrigeration: at least 2 hours

6 large ripe pears, preferably Comice • 2 onions • 2 garlic cloves • 4 tablespoons clarified butter • 250 ml (8 fl oz) dry white wine • 1.5 litres (2½ pints) chicken stock • 250 g (8 oz) blue cheese, preferably Fourme d'Ambert, rind removed • 500 ml (17 fl oz) whipping cream • squeeze of lemon juice (optional) • 1 bunch chives • salt and freshly ground white pepper

Creamy pear soup with blue cheese

• Peel, core and cut the pears into cubes. Peel the onions and garlic and chop finely. Heat the butter in a large saucepan. Add the onions and garlic and cook gently for 3 minutes. Add the pears and sweat for 10 minutes over medium heat. Deglaze the pan with the wine and add the chicken stock. Bring to the boil, then lower the heat, cover and simmer gently for 1 hour.
• Crumble or crush the cheese with a fork. Add to the soup and stir until completely melted. Purée the soup in a blender, then stir in the whipping cream. Season with salt and pepper, and add the lemon juice if desired. Let cool, then refrigerate for at least 2 hours.
• Serve chilled, garnished with snipped chives.
• You can replace the Fourme d'Ambert with any type of blue cheese, such as Stilton or Roquefort.

Brazilian sweet potato soup

• Peel and chop the onion finely. Peel, seed, core and chop the tomatoes. Peel and wash the sweet potatoes, then cut into slices and put them in a casserole with the stock. Bring to the boil. Lower the heat, cover and simmer gently for 20 minutes. Drain and reserve the stock.

• Heat the butter in a saucepan, add the onions and cook over low heat until soft. Add the tomatoes and cook gently for 5 minutes more. Purée in a food processor with the sweet potatoes. Thin with some of the stock if necessary. Return to the pan with the remaining stock. Season and reheat gently.

• Serve hot, garnished with chopped fresh coriander if desired, although this soup is delicious just as it is.

Serves 6
Preparation: 25 minutes
Cooking time: 35 minutes

1 onion
4 ripe tomatoes (or use tinned)
500 g (1 lb) sweet potatoes
(preferably white)
1 litre (1³/₄ pints) beef stock
50 g (2 oz) unsalted butter
1 small bunch fresh coriander
(optional)
salt and freshly ground black
pepper

Mango and melon soup

• Wash and shred the mint leaves, reserving a few for garnish. Wash and peel the mangoes. Remove the stones, holding over a large bowl to catch all the juice. Peel and de-seed the melon and cut into cubes.

• In a food processor, combine the mango, melon, mint, lemon juice, icing sugar, wine and yogurt and process until smooth. Transfer to a bowl and refrigerate for 2 hours.

• Pour into glass bowls and garnish with mint leaves. Serve well chilled, as an entrée.

Serves 4–6
Preparation: 20 minutes
Refrigeration: at least
2 hours

2 sprigs fresh mint
2 ripe mangoes
1 ripe Charentais melon
2 tablespoons lemon juice
1 tablespoon icing sugar
150 ml (¼ pint) dry white wine
2 tablespoons whipped plain yogurt

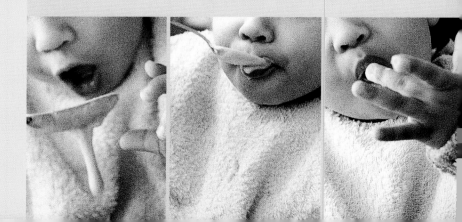

Ivory Coast avocado soup

• Scrub the lime well and cut in half. Squeeze the juice from one half, cut the other half into wafer-thin slices. Wearing rubber gloves to protect your hands, cut the chilli into quarters, core and de-seed. Chop one-quarter to one-half finely (according to taste); slice the remaining pieces thinly. Set aside.

• Cut the avocados in half. Remove the stones, scoop out the flesh with a spoon and put in a food processor. Blend until smooth, Gradually add the stock, mixing between additions. Add the lime juice, yogurt, chopped chilli and a few grindings of pepper. Stir well, cover and refrigerate for at least 1 hour.

• Before serving, taste for seasoning. Transfer into bowls and garnish with slices of lime and chilli.

Note: If your guests (or you) find this dish too hot, instead of using the chopped chillies soak a few chilli slices in the lime juice for 30 minutes. Remove the chilli slices and use the juice as instructed in the recipe. This will give you the chilli flavour, with less of the fire.

Serves 4
Preparation: 30 minutes
Refrigeration: at least 1 hour

1 lime, with bright shiny skin
1 small red, yellow or orange hot chilli, such as Scotch Bonnet or habanero
2 large ripe Haas avocados
1 litre (1³/₄ pints) cold chicken stock
1 tablespoon whipped plain yogurt
salt and freshly ground black pepper

winter soups

Recipe list

Fish soup, Hamburg-style 54

Cream of Jerusalem artichokes with caramelized mushrooms 56

Herb soup, Shaker-style 58

Pumpkin soup with buttery leeks 61

Scotch broth 62

Creamy Hungarian beetroot soup with caraway seeds 64

Belgian onion soup with ale 66

Portuguese cabbage soup (caldo verde) 70

Potato and leek soup, Normandy-style 72

Lentil soup with garlic and tomato (rasam) 75

Cock-a-leekie (Scottish chicken soup) 76

American cheddar and beer soup 77

Fish and okra soup 78

Italian consommé (beef bouillon with egg and parmesan) 80

Hungarian goulash soup 83

Spicy Oriental soup 85

Mexican black bean soup with salsa 86

Columbian chicken soup (ajiaco) 88

Mexican meatball soup 90

Scottish smoked haddock soup 92

introduction

Soup is one of the first 'real' foods most of us encounter, when we graduate from the bottle in babyhood. 'Soup of the evening, beautiful soup' – the word conjures up notions of something soothing, and nourishing, something that makes us grow big and strong. Later, when we are grown (because we ate our soup!), we discover the whole range of soups, with a universe of taste sensations. We learn of broths that are warming and soups that are comforting, served piping hot in warm bowls, with trails of flavoursome steam. The world outside may be dreary, but inside it is warm and comforting. Eaten alone or in company, each spoonful of soup contains a discovery: a small cube of carrot, a slice of mushroom, a tiny piece of pasta, the pearly sheen of seafood in cream, a salty morsel of bacon, a stringy thread of melted cheese. All the flavours mingle gloriously in soupy warmth; we can even make sensual additions such as truffles or porcini. Steaming hot bowls of soup in winter are a blessing to share with good company, when the storms rage outside and the bustle of the day has subsided. Soup is generally eaten in silence, for it demands peaceful contemplation.

Fish soup, Hamburg-style

- Sprinkle the eel pieces with salt and pepper and allow to stand for 2 hours.
- Peel the pears and cut into thin slices. Bring the wine and lemon peel to the boil, add the pear slices and poach until tender. Cover and set aside. In another pan, bring the beef stock to the boil, add the bouquet garni and cauliflower and simmer gently for 15 minutes. Drain the cauliflower and reserve the stock.
- Put the eel in another saucepan and barely cover with cold water. Add the bay leaf, onion and vinegar. Salt, bring to the boil, then simmer gently for 15 minutes. Remove the fish and carefully extract all the bones. Put the boned eel in a soup tureen, with the pears and cauliflower, and keep warm in a low oven.
- Combine together the eel cooking liquid, the reserved beef stock and the pear cooking liquid. Bring to the boil, add the peas and simmer gently for 10–15 minutes. Taste for seasoning. Discard the bouquet garni.
- Mix the egg yolk with a few spoonfuls of hot broth then pour back into the simmering pea mixture. Stir well and pour over the eel.
- Serve hot, accompanied by a wine from Alsace.

Note: The eel skin contributes a great deal of flavour so do not remove it during cooking.

Serves 6
Preparation: 40 minutes
Cooking time: about
45 minutes
Standing time: 2 hours

500 g (1 lb) eel, sliced (or use tuna, swordfish or monkfish)
3 firm, ripe pears
150 ml (¼ pint) dry white wine
1 piece lemon peel
1.5 litres (2½ pints) beef stock
1 bouquet garni (a couple of sprigs each of thyme, tarragon and sage, tied together with kitchen string)
300 g (10 oz) small cauliflower florets
1 bay leaf
1 onion, quartered and sliced
splash of wine vinegar
200 g (7 oz) shelled fresh peas
1 egg yolk
salt and freshly ground pepper

Cream of Jerusalem artichokes with caramelized mushrooms

• Peel the Jerusalem artichokes and the potato and wash. Cut into pieces and place in a pan with the onion and the chicken stock. Bring to the boil, cover and simmer for 30 minutes.

• Meanwhile, trim the mushroom stems and wipe the mushroom caps with damp kitchen paper. Slice the mushroom caps about 5 mm (¼ in) thick.

• Heat the clarified butter in a sauté pan, add the mushroom slices, garlic halves and lemon juice. Cook very gently, until tender, browned and almost caramelized. Season at the end of cooking.

• When the soup is cooked, purée with a hand-held mixer or a blender. Reheat if necessary. Stir in the cream and taste for seasoning.

• Pour into soup bowls and garnish with the caramelized mushrooms and parsley.

Serves 4–6
Preparation: 30 minutes
Cooking time: 35 minutes

500 g (1 lb) Jerusalem artichokes (the less knobbly the better, for easier peeling)

1 new potato

1 onion, sliced

1 litre (1¾ pints) chicken stock

12 chestnut or shiitake mushrooms

4 tablespoons clarified butter or olive oil

1 garlic clove, halved

2 teaspoons lemon juice

120 ml (4 fl oz) double cream

1 small bunch flat-leaf parsley, finely chopped

salt and freshly ground white pepper

Herb soup, Shaker-style

• Peel and wash the potatoes, then cut into quarters. Peel and slice the onions. Put the potatoes and onions in a large pan with enough cold water to cover. Salt lightly and cook over low heat, covered, for 25 minutes. Drain and reserve the cooking liquid. Purée the potato mixture with a food mill or in a blender.

• Heat two-thirds of the milk to boiling, then set aside. Heat the clarified butter in another large saucepan. Add half the parsley, the thyme, savory, marjoram and nettles if using. Add the flour and stir well. Add the remaining cold milk and the sugar, and season.

• Add the hot milk and stir until the liquid begins to thicken. Stir in the potato mixture, adding some of the reserved potato cooking liquid if necessary to thin slightly. Taste for seasoning and heat through.

• Just before serving, stir in the butter, the remaining parsley and the chives.

Serves 6
Preparation: 40 minutes
Cooking time:
about 30 minutes

6 new potatoes
2 onions
750 ml (1¼ pints) whole milk
2 tablespoon clarified butter
6 tablespoons finely chopped
flat-leaf parsley
2 teaspoons fresh thyme leaves,
finely chopped
2 teaspoons fresh marjoram,
finely chopped
1 teaspoon savory or parsley,
finely chopped
6 small, fresh nettle sprigs,
finely chopped (optional, but
use gloves)
2 level tablespoons flour
1 teaspoon sugar
2 tablespoons unsalted butter
3 tablespoons chives, snipped
with scissors
salt and freshly ground white
pepper

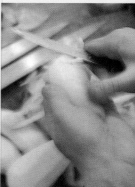

Pumpkin soup with buttery leeks

Serves 4
Preparation:
40 minutes
Cooking time:
about 30 minutes

1 pumpkin (about 700g/ 1½ lb)

1 litre (1¾ pints) chicken stock

2 leeks

50 g (2 oz) clarified butter

a few shavings cheddar or Cantal cheese (optional)

fresh chives, snipped with scissors

salt and freshly ground white pepper

• Cut the pumpkin into largish pieces, then peel and de-seed. Cut the peeled pieces into cubes and put in a saucepan. Add the stock (or water), bring to the boil, then cover and simmer gently for 30 minutes. Drain, reserving the stock. Purée the pumpkin in a blender or with a food mill. Stir into the stock to obtain a thick mixture, adding water if necessary. Taste for seasoning and set aside.

• Wash the leeks and trim, leaving 10 cm (4 inches) of the green end. Slice, but not too thinly. Heat the butter in a pan over medium heat. Add the leek slices and cook until golden, then lower the heat and cook for a few minutes more. They should be just browned and lightly caramelized.

• Reheat the pumpkin soup, adding the leek slices and the cooking butter at the last minute.

• To serve, pour into serving bowls, add a few cheese shavings, if desired, and sprinkle with the chives.

Serves 6–8
Preparation: 30 minutes
Cooking time: about 2 hours
Soaking time: 6 hours

50 g (2 oz) dried chick peas (or 250 g/8 oz fresh shelled peas) • 1 large pinch baking
soda • 750 g (1½ lb) neck of lamb, boned and sliced • 100 g (3½ oz) pearl barley • 1
carrot, finely diced • 1 celery stick, finely diced • 1 turnip, finely diced • 1 large onion,
finely chopped • 1 bouquet garni (parsley, bay leaf and thyme or savory) •
2 large leeks, with a bit of green • 8 sprigs flat leaf parsley • 3 sprigs fresh mint •
50 g (2 oz) unsalted butter • 1 lemon, quartered • salt, coarsely ground pepper and
freshly ground pepper

Scotch broth

• If using chick peas, soak for 6 hours in enough cold water to cover, along with the baking soda.

• Bring 1.5 litres (3 pints) of water to the boil in a large saucepan. Salt lightly and add the lamb. Return to the boil, skimming frequently to remove any foam, then add the drained chick peas and the pearl barley. Stir well.

• Bring back to the boil, then add the carrots, celery, turnip, onion, bouquet garni and coarse pepper. Lower the heat, cover and simmer gently until the meat is tender, about 1½ hours. Remove the lamb with a slotted spoon. If using fresh peas, add them at this point and continue cooking.

• Meanwhile, cut the meat into small pieces and return to the soup. Taste and adjust seasoning and simmer for a further 10 minutes.

• Cut the leek into 1 cm (½ inch) thick slices and chop the green part finely. Chop the parsley and mint finely. Add the white leek slices to the soup and simmer for a further 5 minutes. Remove from the heat and stir in the leek greens, parsley, mint and butter. Stir well.

• Serve with some crusty bread and lemon quarters for squeezing, as desired.

Creamy Hungarian beetroot soup with caraway seeds

• Chop the onion finely. Cut the beetroot into fine dice. Heat the goose or duck fat in a large saucepan over medium heat, add the onion and caraway seeds and cook, stirring constantly, for 5 minutes. When the onion is soft but not browned, add the teaspoon of paprika and cook, stirring for a few seconds; do not burn. Add the beetroot, stir, then add the beef stock. Bring gently to the boil and cook over low heat for 10 minutes.

Serves 6
Preparation: 25 minutes
Cooking time: 15 minutes

1 small onion
4 cooked beetroot, peeled
1 tablespoon goose or duck fat
or olive oil
1/2 teaspoon caraway seeds
1 teaspoon Hungarian paprika
1 litre (1 3/4 pints) beef stock
1 tablespoon flour
4 tablespoons crème fraîche
3–4 tablespoons vinegar

• **For the garnish:**
chives snipped with scissors,
crème fraîche, chopped walnuts,
Hungarian paprika

• Meanwhile, combine the flour and crème fraîche in a bowl. Stir well and add the vinegar to thin. Add water, if necessary, to thin further. Set aside.

• Purée the beet soup in a blender or with a food mill. Return to the heat and stir in the crème fraîche mixture. Bring gently to simmering point, stirring, and cook for a minute over a low heat.

• Serve hot, garnished with chives, crème fraîche, chopped walnuts and paprika.

Belgian onion soup with ale

• Peel and thinly slice the onions. Heat the butter in a large saucepan, add the onions and cook gently until soft. Add the stock and ale and season. Cook and simmer gently for 30 minutes. Taste for seasoning.

• Preheat the grill. Put the slices of bread on a baking sheet and grill on both sides until golden. Cover with the grated cheese and grill until the cheese is melted and lightly browned.

• Ladle the soup into bowls and top each with a slice of toasted bread. Serve immediately.

Serves 4
Preparation: 30 minutes
Cooking time: 30 minutes

2 large red onions
6 tablespoons clarified butter
500 ml (17 fl oz) chicken or beef stock
750 ml (1¼ pints) bière de garde (strong Belgian beer), or strong ale
4 thick slices rustic bread
6 heaped tablespoons grated Parmesan (or Gruyère)
salt and freshly ground pepper

Helpful hints
for winter

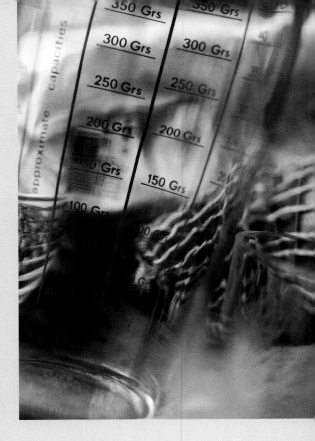

As soon as the first frost appears, it's time for robust soups based on beans, dried peas and lentils. In order to get the best from these ingredients, be sure to allow adequate steeping and cooking time. Add baking soda to the soaking-water; this will tenderize them even further and shorten the soaking time. This works especially well for chick-peas. Rinse carefully and cook in fresh water. The outer skins of chick-peas can be removed by rubbing them between your fingers, after soaking. When cooking any kind of bean, use filtered water, or spring water with a low mineral content, which will help to tenderize them even more; hard water should be avoided when cooking beans. Finally, check the use-by date on all packages. Fresh beans will give the best result and, ideally, you should use beans harvested in the year of use. When cooking with stock, salt lightly, or not at all; the important thing is to taste regularly during cooking. Lemon juice can partially replace salt, so use salt moderately when preparing a soup with lemon juice.

• Stock made from poultry or meat can be refrigerated without degreasing, but do not leave it for more than 3 days before skimming off the fat. Concentrated stock cubes can also be made by reducing stocks as much as desired (do not over-season if reducing a great deal) and freezing in ice cube trays.

• **Chicken stock:** chicken carcass (raw or cooked, with giblets) or a whole chicken, bouquet garni, whole peppercorns, small slice of ginger, a few vegetables (onion, celery, tomato, etc – optional). Cover the chicken with water and bring to the boil, skimming any foam that rises to the surface, then lower the heat, add the remaining ingredients, salt lightly and simmer gently, covered, for 2½ hours.

• **Beef or veal stock:** 1 kg (2 lb) braising beef with bones, or veal shanks, bouquet garni, whole peppercorns, small slice of ginger, onion, garlic, carrots, celery, etc. Prepare as for the chicken stock. Cook for 3–4 hours, covered, simmering gently.

Portuguese cabbage soup (caldo verde)

• Peel the potatoes and chop the onion and garlic finely. Heat some olive oil in a large saucepan, add the onion and garlic and cook until soft and just browning. Add the potatoes and cook, stirring, for 2 minutes. Add 1.5 litres (3 pints) water and bring to the boil, then lower the heat, cover and simmer gently until the potatoes are tender, about 25 minutes.

Serves 6
Preparation: 30 minutes
Cooking time:
about 30 minutes

6 new potatoes
1 large onion
1 large garlic clove
olive oil
150 g (5 oz) Spanish or Portuguese chorizo, sliced
400 g (13 oz) spring greens, Chinese leaf, Savoy cabbage or turnip greens
salt and freshly ground black pepper

• Heat some olive oil in a frying pan, add the chorizo slices and cook for a few minutes. Set aside. Wash the cabbage and drain well.

• Mash the potatoes thoroughly into the cooking liquid or use a potato ricer, add the chorizo slices, season with salt and pepper and continue to cook over low heat.

• Meanwhile, roll up the cabbage leaves like a Swiss roll, a few at a time, then slice crosswise to obtain a julienne. Add to the soup and cook for a few minutes until tender or al dente, according to your own taste.

• Serve with olive oil and sliced rustic bread.

Potato and leek soup, Normandy-style

• Wash the leeks thoroughly and trim, leaving about 7 cm (3 inches) of the green. Peel and dice the potatoes. Slice the leek whites thinly and reserve the green part. Put the leek whites and potatoes into a large pan, add 1 litre (1¾ pints) of water and bring to the boil. Salt lightly. Cover, lower the heat and simmer gently for 30 minutes.

• Purée the soup in a food mill, taste for seasoning and return to low heat.

• Slice the green parts of the leeks thinly. Bring the soup to a light boil, add the leek greens, cover and remove from the heat. Allow to stand for 5 minutes.

• Ladle into bowls, top with a knob of butter or a dollop of cream and some ground pepper and serve with crusty, fresh bread.

Serves 4-6
Preparation: 30 minutes
Cooking time:
30 minutes

4 large leeks
4 potatoes (about 500 g/1 lb)
unsalted butter, or thick cream
salt and freshly ground pepper

Serves 4–6
Preparation: 1 hour
Cooking time: 1 hour 30 minutes

200 g (7 oz) toor dal (yellow split lentils) • ½ **lime, scrubbed** • **1 teaspoon ground turmeric** • **1 large piece of dried tamarind** • **4 tablespoons clarified butter** • **1 tablespoon + 1 teaspoon cumin seeds** • **10 large garlic cloves** • **1 large ripe tomato** • **2 tablespoons coriander seeds** • ¼ **tablespoon black peppercorns** • **1 dried red chilli** • **1 pinch asafoetida (available from Indian stores)** • **fresh coriander leaves, shredded** • **salt** • **For the garnish: 2 garlic cloves, sliced** • **8 curry leaves** • **1 teaspoon black mustard seeds** • ½ **teaspoon cumin seeds** • **2 tablespoons white mustard seeds**

Lentil soup with garlic and tomato (rasam)

• Rinse the lentils thoroughly. Put them in a large pot with enough water to cover them by about 3 cm (1 inch). Add the lime half and the turmeric and bring to the boil. Cook until the lentils are tender, about 1 hour. Drain, reserving the cooking liquid. Discard the lime half. Crush the lentils, then stir them into the reserved liquid.

• Soak the tamarind in hot water for 5 minutes then press through a fine sieve to extract the pulp.

• Heat some of the clarified butter. Add 1 teaspoon of the cumin seeds and the whole peeled garlic cloves and cook until just golden. Peel, de-seed and finely chop the tomato. Add to the garlic and cumin mixture and purée in a blender.

• With a coffee grinder, grind together the coriander seeds, peppercorns, the remaining cumin seeds and the chilli. In a pan, combine the ground spices, tamarind pulp, asafoetida and some salt. Bring to the boil. Stir in the tomato mixture, then the lentils and their liquid. Thin with water if necessary. Taste for seasoning and simmer gently for 30 minutes.

• For the garnish: heat the remaining clarified butter, add the remaining garnish ingredients and cook until golden. Bring the soup back to the boil and stir in the garnish mixture, then remove from the heat and allow to stand for 3 minutes.

• Serve, sprinkled with shredded coriander leaves.

Cock-a-leekie (Scottish chicken soup)

Serves 6
Preparation: 30 minutes
Cooking time: about 2 hours

2 litres (3¼ pints) chicken stock (or water) • 8 large leeks • 1 free-range chicken, about 1 kg (2 lb) • 10 black peppercorns • 8 allspice berries • 2 whole cloves • 1 pinch ground mace • 3 sprigs flat leaf parsley • 12 plump Agen prunes, unstoned

• Bring the stock (or water) to the boil. Meanwhile, wash the leeks thoroughly and trim, leaving 5 cm (2 inches) at the green end. Slice 3 of the leeks finely. When the stock comes to the boil, add the chicken and the sliced leeks. Tie all the spices and the parsley in a small square of muslin and tie securely. Add the spice bundle to the cooking chicken. Cover, lower the heat and simmer gently for 1½ hours. Degrease by blotting the surface with kitchen paper.

• Cut the remaining leeks into 2.5 cm (1 inch) rounds; chop a bit of the green end finely and put to one side for garnish.

• Add the prunes (with stones intact) to the soup. Bring to a gentle boil and continue cooking for 20 minutes. Turn off the heat, remove the chicken and cut into serving pieces. Add the rounds of leek to the soup, cover, and allow to stand for 3 minutes.

• Serve the chicken pieces alongside the soup, on a separate platter, or put some sliced chicken into each serving bowl and fill with broth, leek pieces and a couple of prunes. Garnish with a sprinkling of chopped leek greens.

Serves 6–8
Preparation: 30 minutes
Cooking time: 30 minutes

1 large carrot • 1 celery stick • 1 large onion • 750 ml
(1¼ pints) beer (lager, ale or Trappist) • 2 tablespoons
chicken stock powder • 2 tablespoons flour • 750 ml
(1¼ pints) milk • 500 g (1 lb) mature cheddar, grated or
crumbled • salt and freshly ground pepper

American cheddar and beer soup

• Peel the carrot and slice thinly lengthwise (julienne). Cut the celery in a fine dice. Peel and finely chop the onion.

• Combine the beer and chicken stock powder in a large saucepan. Bring slowly to the boil, stirring occasionally, then add the carrot, celery and onion. Cover and simmer gently for 10 minutes

• In a small bowl, mix the flour with one-third of the milk, adding it little by little. Gradually pour this into the soup, whisking continuously, until it is completely incorporated.

• Add the remaining milk and return to the boil. Lower the heat and cook until the soup begins to thicken slightly, about 15 minutes. Gradually add the cheese, stirring well between each addition to melt thoroughly. Season generously and cook very gently for a minute more.

• Serve immediately, with slices of crusty baguette.

Fish and okra soup

- Salt the fish fillets and cut into large pieces. Slice the eel and sprinkle with lime juice. Set aside. Wash the okra, trim the stem end and slice thinly into rounds.
- Place the stock in a large pan, add one chilli quarter, the tomatoes, okra and the bicarbonate of soda and bring to the boil. Simmer gently, uncovered for 10–15 minutes. Add the eel. Chop the spinach coarsely and add to the soup, salt, then cover and allow to simmer gently for 20 minutes. Meanwhile, skin and remove the bones from the smoked mackerel and flake the flesh into large pieces.
- Taste the soup for seasoning. Add the fish pieces, smoked mackerel and remaining chilli. Simmer gently for 3–5 minutes. Remove from the heat and stir in the palm oil, mixing gently to incorporate.
- Serve with rice.

Serves 6
Preparation: 1 hour
Cooking time: 35 minutes

500 g (1 lb) white fish fillets (haddock, hake, halibut, cod, sole, plaice etc)

300 g (10 oz) eel

Juice of ½ lime

400 g (13 oz) okra

500 ml (17 fl oz) fresh, strong fish or beef stock

1 Scotch bonnet or habanero chilli, de-seeded and quartered

1 x 400g (13 oz) tin chopped peeled tomatoes

pinch of bicarbonate of soda

250 g (8 oz) fresh spinach, washed and trimmed

1 smoked mackerel

250 ml (8 fl oz) red palm oil (zomi, available in African speciality shops)

salt and freshly ground pepper

- **To serve:**
cooked white rice

Italian consommé (beef bouillon with egg and Parmesan)

• Preheat the oven to 180°C (350°F), gas mark 4. Heat the butter in a frying pan and add the bread slices, cooking until brown on both sides. Put one slice in each serving bowl and place in the warm oven.

Serves 6
Preparation: 30 minutes
Cooking time:
10 minutes

4 tablespoons clarified butter
6 slices rustic sourdough bread
(such as Poilâne)
1.5 litres (2½ pints) strong beef
or chicken stock
6 fresh eggs
6 heaped tablespoons grated
Parmesan cheese
flat leaf parsley, finely chopped
grated nutmeg
salt and freshly ground pepper

• Bring the stock to the boil and taste for seasoning.

• Remove the bowls from the oven. Break an egg onto each of the bread slices, then pour over the boiling stock. Season with pepper. Stand for 3 minutes to allow the egg white to harden, then sprinkle generously with Parmesan, chopped parsley and nutmeg. Serve immediately.

Hungarian goulash soup

• Cut the meat into 2.5 cm (1 inch) cubes; chop the onions coarsely. Heat the lard or butter in a large cast-iron casserole. Add the onions and cook until translucent, about 10 minutes. Add the meat and cook for 10 minutes more.

• Crush the garlic with the caraway seeds and some salt. Remove the casserole from the heat and stir in the garlic paste and the paprika, mixing well. Add 2 litres (3½ pints) water, cover and simmer gently for 1 hour.

• Peel, de-seed and chop the tomato. Wash and slice the pepper. Add both to the soup, taste for seasoning, add more water if necessary and simmer for a further 30 minutes.

• Peel and wash the potatoes, then cut into large cubes. Add these to the soup and cook until tender, about 20 minutes more. Taste for seasoning.

• Serve in deep soup bowls with crusty bread and a good red wine.

Serves 6
Preparation: 30 minutes
Cooking time: just over 2 hours

1 kg (2 lb) braising steak
2 large onions
2 tablespoons lard or clarified butter
1 garlic clove
pinch caraway seeds
3 tablespoons mild Hungarian paprika (or 2 tablespoons mild and 1 tablespoon hot)
1 large ripe tomato
1 red or green pepper
500 g (1 lb) new potatoes
salt

Spicy oriental soup

Serves 6
Preparation: 50 minutes
Cooking time: 12–15
minutes

36 dried lily buds (available
from Asian stores)
6 large dried Chinese
mushrooms
1 handful dried Chinese
mushrooms, such as tree ears
1 boneless chicken breast
1 egg
groundnut and sesame oil
1 x 5 mm (¼ inch) thick slice
fresh ginger root, chopped
1 tablespoon soy sauce
2 tablespoons Chinese cooking
wine
1 litre (1¾ pints) chicken stock
2 tablespoons cornflour diluted
in 4 tablespoons water
1 piece firm tofu, cubed
100 g (3½ oz) raw prawns,
peeled and chopped
1 spring onion, chopped
salt

• For the marinade:
1 tablespoon soy sauce
1 tablespoon Chinese
cooking wine
1 teaspoon sugar
1 teaspoon cornflour
1 tablespoon sesame oil

• For the sweet-sour sauce:
2 tablespoons red wine vinegar
1 tablespoon soy sauce
1 teaspoon ground white
pepper
2 teaspoons chilli oil
1 tablespoon sesame oil

• Make the marinade and the sweet-sour sauce by combining all the ingredients in two small bowls. Set aside.

• Put the lily buds and mushrooms in separate bowls and add hot water to cover. Soak for 30 minutes to soften. Drain and clean them all, and trim the hard tips of the lily buds. Slice the mushrooms. Cut the chicken into thin slices, then toss in the marinade and set aside. Beat the egg with a little sesame oil.

• Heat some groundnut oil in a wok over high heat. Add the ginger and chicken, season and cook, stirring for a minute. Remove the chicken and add the mushrooms and lily buds. Cook, stirring, for 1 minute, then add the soy sauce, wine and stock. Bring to the boil, then lower the heat and simmer for 10 minutes.

• Raise the heat, add the diluted cornflour and cook until the soup thickens. Remove from the heat and gently stir in the beaten egg. Add the tofu, chicken and prawn pieces.

• Pour half of the sauce into a soup tureen, fill with the soup and top with the remaining sauce. Garnish with chopped spring onion and serve.

Serves 6
Preparation: 30 minutes
Cooking time: 2 hours 45 minutes

300 g (10 oz) Mexican black beans (the long ones) • pinch of baking soda • pinch
ground cumin • 2 pinches oregano • 1 bay leaf • 4 bottled jalapeño peppers • 4 ripe
tomatoes • 3 large garlic cloves • 3 onions • 1 large bunch fresh coriander, washed
and dried• 1 celery stick • 1 tablespoon red wine vinegar • 2 tablespoons olive oil •
4 tablespoons dry sherry • salt and freshly ground pepper

Mexican black bean soup with salsa

• Rinse and pick over the beans. Place in a large casserole, add plenty of cold water and the baking soda and bring to the boil. Boil for 5 minutes, then add the cumin, oregano and bay leaf. Cover and simmer gently for 1 hour.

• Chop 2 of the jalapeños finely and add to the beans. Cook for a further 1–1½ hours, adding more water if necessary. Season lightly.

• Peel, de-seed and finely chop the tomatoes. Peel and finely chop the garlic and onion, along with the coriander, celery and the remaining chillies.

• For the salsa, combine in a bowl half the tomatoes, one-third of the onions and garlic, all the coriander, chillies and the wine vinegar. Season liberally with salt and pepper. Cover and set aside.

• When the beans are tender, remove from the stove. Heat some olive oil in a pan, add the remaining onion and garlic and cook for 5 minutes. Add the celery and the rest of the tomatoes and cook, uncovered for 10 minutes, to reduce.

• Purée half the bean soup, then stir in the tomato mixture. Stir this into the remaining bean soup, add the sherry and stir well. Taste for seasoning.

• Serve with a dollop of salsa in the middle of each bowl, accompanied by some fresh bread.

Columbian chicken soup (ajiaco)

• Slice the onions. Peel and wash the potatoes, cut the large potatoes into thin slices and set aside. Put the baby potatoes in cold water and set aside.

• In a large casserole, heat the butter or oil. Add the chicken pieces and onions and cook until golden. Add the potato slices and the stock. Bring to the boil, then lower the heat and simmer gently for 25 minutes. Add the baby potatoes and cook for a further 20 minutes.

• Remove the chicken pieces and the baby potatoes from the soup. Purée the soup (or force through a sieve) and return to the casserole. Taste for seasoning, then return the chicken and baby potatoes to the soup. Add the undrained corn kernels and the capers. Simmer for 5 minutes, then, just before serving, stir in the whipping cream.

• Crush the avocado flesh and mix with the chopped egg yolk. Add the remaining sauce ingredients and mix well.

• Serve the soup with the avocado sauce on the side.

Serves 4
Preparation: 40 minutes
Cooking time:
about 1 hour

2 large onions
500 g (1 lb) baby new potatoes
4 large red or new potatoes
50 g (2 oz) clarified butter or olive oil
1 free-range chicken (about 1.2 kg/2½ lb), cut into 8 pieces, or 1 kg (2 lb) chicken thighs, cut into pieces
2 litres (3½ pints) chicken stock
2 tins sweetcorn kernels, yellow or white (500g/1 lb total)
3 tablespoons capers
125 ml (4 fl oz) whipping cream
salt and freshly ground pepper

• **For the avocado sauce:**
1 large ripe Haas avocado
1 hard-boiled egg, white and yolk chopped separately
1 spring onion, finely chopped
2 tablespoons finely chopped fresh coriander
¼ Habanero chilli, finely chopped, or more to taste
1 tablespoon white wine vinegar
salt and pepper

Mexican meatball soup

- Peel, de-seed and chop the tomato. Peel the onion and chop finely. Heat some olive oil in a pan, add the onions and cook over medium heat until golden. Add the tomato, chilli, sugar and a pinch each of salt and pepper. Cook until thick.
- Soak the breadcrumbs in milk for a few seconds, then squeeze dry. Mix with the veal, sultanas, a pinch of grated nutmeg, the Parmesan and the warm tomato sauce. Add the eggs and mix until thoroughly combined. Shape into balls about 3–5 cm (1–2 inches) in diameter and set aside.
- To prepare the broth: cook the onion in a little olive oil until soft, then add the stock, wine and seasonings and boil for a few minutes. Season with salt and pepper, then carefully add the meatballs. Cover and simmer gently for 40 minutes. Add more stock or wine if the liquid reduces too much.
- Serve in soup bowls, garnished with chopped coriander.

Serves 4
Preparation: 1 hour
Cooking time:
40-50 minutes

• For the meatballs:
1 ripe tomato
1 onion
olive oil
1 bottled jalapeño chilli, finely chopped
1 teaspoon sugar
60 g (2½ oz) fine breadcrumbs
a little milk (if necessary)
500 g (1 lb) minced veal
60 g (2¼ oz) sultanas
4 tablespoons grated Parmesan cheese
2 eggs
fresh chopped coriander
salt, freshly ground pepper, and grated nutmeg

• For the broth:
1 onion, finely chopped
750 ml (1¼ pints) beef stock
300 ml (½ pint) good red wine
1 large pinch dried thyme
1 large pinch dried oregano
1 bay leaf

Scottish smoked haddock soup

• Chop the onion very finely. Heat the butter in a pan, add the onion and cook over low heat until soft, about 5 minutes. Cut the haddock into large pieces, keeping the skin on and add to the onions. Add enough water to just cover, bring to the boil, then cover and simmer gently for 8 minutes. Peel and wash the potatoes, cut into large pieces and boil or steam until cooked through.

• Remove the fish from the soup and set aside to cool. Save the cooking liquid. Mash the potatoes finely with a potato ricer until smooth. Remove the bones and skin from the haddock, then flake the flesh finely.

• Gradually stir the haddock cooking liquid into the mashed potatoes, then stir in the milk, followed by the haddock pieces. If the soup is too thick, add a little more water. Bring to the boil, then lower the heat and simmer gently for 10 minutes. Taste for seasoning, add a generous grinding of pepper and stir in the parsley. Allow to stand for 3 minutes.

• Serve hot, garnished with chives and with a knob of butter or a dollop of crème fraîche in each bowl.

Serves 4
Preparation: 25 minutes
Cooking time: 18 minutes

1 onion
4 tablespoons clarified butter
1 smoked haddock fillet, about 500 g (1 lb)
2 large new potatoes (about 350 g/12 oz)
400 ml (14 fl oz) milk (or half whipping cream, half water)
chopped flat leaf parsley, chives snipped with scissors
dreshly ground pepper
unsalted butter or crème fraîche, for serving

index of recipes

Almond gazpacho 33

American cheddar and beer soup 77

Andalucian hake soup 28

Belgian onion soup with ale 66

Brazilian sweet potato soup 44

Chilled rocket soup 20

Cock-a-leekie (Scottish chicken soup) 76

Columbian chicken soup (ajiaco) 88

Cream of cucumber with mint 10

Cream of Jerusalem artichokes with caramelized mushrooms 56

Creamy Hungarian beetroot soup with caraway seeds 64

Creamy Mexican courgette soup 17

Creamy pear soup with blue cheese 42

Fish and okra soup 78

Fish soup, Hamburg-style 54

French fish soup (bourride) 36

Greek egg soup with lemon 31

Herb soup, Shaker-style 58

Hungarian chicken and white grape soup 32

Hungarian goulash soup 83

Hungarian sour cherry soup 34

Indian tomato soup 41

Italian consommé (beef bouillon with egg and parmesan) 80

Ivory Coast avocado soup 48

Jellied beetroot consommé 12

Lentil soup with garlic and tomato (rasam) 75

Mango and melon soup 46

Mexican black bean soup with salsa 86

Mexican meatball soup 90

Normandy apple and potato soup 26

Portuguese cabbage soup (caldo verde) 70

Potato and leek soup, Normandy-style 72

Provençal vegetable soup (soupe au pistou) 18

Pumpkin soup with buttery leeks 61

Scotch broth 62

Scottish smoked haddock soup 92

Senegalese prawn soup with coconut 39

Spicy Oriental soup 85

Strawberry soup with balsamic vinegar 22

Vichyssoise with watercress 14